RARE, WILD

and FREE

Also by Mike Tomkies

Books

Nature
Alone in the Wilderness
Between Earth and Paradise
A Last Wild Place
My Wilderness Wildcats
Liane – A Cat from the Wild
Wildcat Haven
Out of the Wild
Golden Eagle Years
On Wing and Wild Water
Moobli
Last Wild Years
In Spain's Secret Wilderness
Wildcats
Rare, Wild and Free

Biography

The Big Man (The John Wayne Story)
It Sure Beats Working (The Robert Mitchum Story)

Unpublished Novels

Let Ape and Tiger Die
Today the Wolf is Dead

Autobiography

My Wicked First Life

Videos

Eagle Mountain Year
At Home with Eagles
Forest Phantoms
My Barn Owl Family
River Dancing Year
Wildest Spain
Wildest Spain Revisited
Last Eagle Years
My Bird Table Theatres
My Wild 75th Summer
My Wild 80th Year (In preparation)

RARE, WILD

---

and FREE

Mike Tomkies

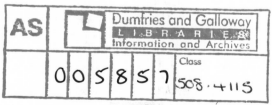

WHITTLES PUBLISHING

Published by
Whittles Publishing,
Dunbeath,
Caithness KW6 6EY,
Scotland, UK
www.whittlespublishing.com

© 2008 Mike Tomkies
ISBN 978-1904445-51-7

Typesetting and layout by Mark Mechan

Printed in Malta by Progress Press Company Ltd.

Mike Tomkies

Naturalist, author and film-maker, Mike Tomkies has inspired a huge amount of people through his books and films on wildlife and conservation and is an Honorary Fellow of the Royal Zoological Society of Scotland. He has spent most of the last 40 years in wild remote places in Canada, Scotland and Spain, mostly with only access by boat and without electricity, gas, mains water, postal delivery, telephone or even a road. He studied the last truly wild places, man's effect on them, and in his books made detailed and often unique observations of some of the world's rarest wildlife.

Originally a country journalist who made it to Fleet Street and then to Hollywood, where he knew the major movie stars well, in his late 30s he turned his back on the fast lane to devote his life to studying and writing about rare and endangered wildlife.

Leaving his former showbiz lifestyle behind, he set off virtually penniless from Hollywood to Vancouver in a rickety old milk truck and built himself a log cabin in the Canadian wilderness. Living alone and mainly off the sea, he began his wildlife studies with grizzly bears, cougars, bald eagles and killer whales. The resulting book, *Alone In The Wilderness*, took him three years to write and was snapped up by Reader's Digest. From Canada he moved to remote parts of the Scottish Highlands, again living largely from the land and sea around him, where he studied, photographed and wrote about the rarest Scottish wildlife, most notably the golden eagle, black throated diver, pine marten and wildcat. He was the first person to breed wildcats successfully and release them to the wild. For over 20 years he slogged up and down sea and fresh water lochs in small open boats in all weathers to reach his primitive isolated homes. An expert field-worker, he lived closer to rare wildlife than anyone had for many years, trekking, stalking and spending up to 38 hours at a time in his 'invisible' home-made hides, notching up a total of more than 3,000 hours over the years.

During his five years in the wilds of Spain, to be where the rarest wildlife existed, he lived in a crumbling old villa with no glass in its windows, and not even a water supply: every two weeks he climbed up the mountain to fill plastic containers from a spring.

On the rare occasions when he did meet 'establishment' conservationists, comments were often made about how privileged he was to live and work in such wild situations. The fact is that while doing the same sort of work as other naturalists, unlike them he had no organisational backup, no salary or grant, no electricity, and no road access to his remote homes. At the end of a hard, cold trekking day he had to get home and chop wood for a fire, make his food by oil lamp, tend his boat and home and generally work twice as hard as the others.

When he was not rowing his boat or climbing mountains ('Not to reach their summits but to learn their wildlife secrets'), Tomkies bred, studied and released to the wild nine ferocious wildcats. His four books about his studies and personal adventures with these rare, fierce and intractable creatures are perhaps best epitomized in his book, *Wildcat Haven*. His remarkable rapport with the wild animals around him, such as the pine marten family which came through his window every night for tasty tidbits, or the owls, foxes and badgers that he nursed through injury in his home before returning to the wild, is revealed in his book, *Out of the Wild*.

At the age of 56, Mike bought an old movie camera and began slogging over his mountains with a 60 lb pack. He has since made ten full-length videos of rare wildlife which, like his books, have given pleasure to thousands. His work and way of life was featured in a 1977 BBC documentary *Keeper Of The Wild* which was well received. In 1988 he was elected an Honorary Fellow of the Royal Zoological Society of Scotland. In 1989, trying to sell some of his own wildlife film, Scottish TV talked him into making another half-hour programme, *Wild Cathedral*. This was so successful it was main networked twice, then repeated five times on regional channels, breaking the record for an STV half-hour documentary. A setback came in 1996 when he underwent an operation for colon cancer but he just kept on trekking and filming and after his last annual checkup his doctors told him he was in the clear.

Mike is still working with wildlife both in Scotland and Spain, including trekking miles to film remote sea eagles on his 76th birthday. He needed final scenes for his third film on eagles to add to his three books on the same species. It was mainly for his work on eagles and pioneering breeding of rare wildcats that he was honoured by the Royal Zoological Society of Scotland almost 20 years ago. He is now working on his eleventh wildlife video about nature in the South Downs – in his 80th year Mike Tomkies treks and climbs on …

On his best-selling book *A Last Wild Place*, the Duke of Edinburgh said:
"The North West of Scotland is indeed a wild place, but to the observant eye of the author it is full of wonderful life. This book does more than describe a piece of wild country and its population of wild animals: it gives a vivid picture of someone totally absorbed by his subject."

From the *Sunday Express*:
"There is a stark but joyful timelessness about Mike Tomkies' book, a vibrant awe at the miracles and mysteries of Nature and a certainty that Man, despite his cities and sophistication, is only a small part of that magic."

From the *Sunday Times*:
"A beautiful book about a beautiful place, written with grace and humility …"

On the first of his three eagle books, *Golden Eagle Years*, Brian Jackman wrote:
"… it is a triumph of personal observation, a wilderness saga told by a true craftsman with honesty, fervour and an unerring eye for detail … an unrivalled insight into the lives of these magnificent birds of prey."

"…The excellent Mike Tomkies … gives us another book about his life among the free wild creatures of the Scottish Highlands. …With infinite tact, delicacy and soggy labour he has kept a gentle eye on his local eyries, and spent long hours in such intimate contact with their inhabitants that once a gigantic female, sweeping down to her chicks, actually touched the top of his head in passing." *The Times*

"… his best book to date … the extraordinary account of eight tough, gruelling but splendid years watching eagles in the West Highlands … contains brilliant descriptions of Highland country and, of course, of the marvellous birds he was studying." *The Scots Magazine*

In Spain's Secret Wilderness

This was the first full work on that country's major wildlife species for over 100 years, and of it the *Sunday Express* said:

" … he describes the extraordinary terrain, his lengthy travels tracking and photographing the wild animals – and what a fascinating, almost alluring, world it proved to be. He found rare birds – the mighty lammergeier for instance, and the Imperial eagle, not to mention the black stork and other species that are now almost extinct in other parts of Europe. He found the isolated haunts of creatures like the Spanish ibex, the mongoose, wild boar, bear, wolf and lynx … He writes of it all with infectious enthusiasm, guiding us confidently into a world of nature we can hardly believe still exists in western Europe."

Britain's top wildlife photographer Laurie Campbell cites Mike as a big hero. Over 5,000 people have written to him, many saying his books and films had not only changed the way they looked at the natural world but the way they looked at life itself. He treasures every letter.

'Early Revelations from the wild'

– an excerpt from Alone in the Wilderness by the author, written in 1975

I had been living in the Pacific coastal wilds of Canada for two years when I had a strange experience …

There are rare moments in the wilderness when one's feelings are like none you have ever known before – they seem new and original – as if one had shed one's old self and grown a new one. The behaviour patterns built up over years of civilised living, and all the adjustments one has had to make from the innocent integrity of childhood to cope, survive, and succeed, have all been cut away. It is as if one has broken through some opaque spiritual barrier.

One afternoon I was swimming in the warm, gleaming sea of my bay, with all conscious thought processes suspended. I was just gliding along the crystal-smooth surface when quite suddenly I felt I no longer had a separate identity. My feeling of self, of being separated from the whole, had now become a delusion of the past. I looked at the island rocks shimmering in the heat and I was their granite hardness, at the treetops being stirred by gentle breezes and I could feel the winds sifting through my own body, at the slowly unfolding shapes of the tangleweed below me whose movements in the water also seemed to be my own. I felt strangely at one with them all and with all life, that, indeed, I was at one with all things everywhere. And I felt, too, a strange power that I could do anything I wished in the water. I began to swim without effort, to travel through the water with the minimum of movement and for a great distance with complete ease. It was as if I had actually become a fish or a seal, completely at one with a cherishing sea, able to progress by merely willing it. The experience was too profound to doubt.

During this strange interlude I saw a line of wild guillemots swimming ahead near some drifting kelp, and I found I could move toward them without a ripple; from quite a distance away I submerged quietly, sliding under the weed, and came up beneath them, seizing the nearest by a bright red leg. The moment I did, it flapped and squawked, and as I let it go and the birds took off, their wings whirring like little black clockwork toys, my normal consciousness returned and the spell was broken. I was instantly aware again of only my *self* and as I was now over a mile from the beach, I felt a panicky awareness of danger, and my return swim entailed much effort. Since then there have been similar experiences of intensified perception, exhilaration, of lost and ancient senses, of exaltation even, but such words are inadequate and cannot really convey the truth of the experiences. A feeling of being totally *alive* perhaps. Like so many of us, I often go through life without really living, like a deaf, blind, thoughtless being intent only upon my personal problems, without ever really being *there*. But during these strange, all too few moments, it has seemed as if, alone with nature for long periods, I have become blessed with occasional glimpses of a true cosmic harmony.

For years I had sought a basic code by which I might try to live, although in the cities it had become buried. But now, in tranquil moments alone and after all the experiences in the wild, this desire suddenly returned with redoubled force. Amid the rocky arbours, the dark temples below the cedar trees, I found myself staring at the ancient granite as if buried in this aged landscape I might find an answer. Every religion or philosophy I had studied seemed only to provide hints that when organised, structured, and tailored for large masses of people often became reduced to a ritualised system of dogmatic assertions.

Although I'd never been a complete atheist, I had hidden for years behind the skirts of agnosticism, asserting that for man complete knowledge of an infinite, omniscient God was impossible. But during the years in the wild, especially when trekking through mountainous bear country far from man, I had several times felt there were mysterious forces at work, both malign and benign. Often, when first seeing an animal that could kill me, I had muttered a silent prayer, hoping as I wished no ill to the creature, that I would thus be in tune with the benign forces. And when you come near to losing your life in rough seas, and for long periods are exposed to both elemental winter dangers and the glories of beatific summer days, observing all the while the pageantry of natural life, it seems impossible any longer not to believe in a creator of some kind beyond all. Yet today we are no nearer to understanding God than were the ancients, for man's finite mind will never satisfactorily define the Infinite. We may feel, sense, have faith, but we continue to stagger blindly. The primitive native beliefs that Tihoni had expounded so clearly – of many gods for the seas, rivers, forests, and mountains, all linked to the Great Spirit, may seem simplistic or mere superstition to most of us. But surely our concepts of a personalised and selective God whose will manifests itself in the destinies of chosen people, who watches the individual lives of billions at the same time, who punishes and rewards according to the degree of obedience, who dismisses the animal creation, even demands animal sacrifices, is no better? For months I had tried to understand this creative benign force I had often sensed, a force that lay far beyond mere goodness itself, and to strip away the heavenly props and petty dogmas of traditional organised religions.

On the afternoon that I returned from my strange swim I found my mind struggling again with these ideas, when I felt a sudden terror that in trying to delve too deeply into meanings I was approaching some spiritual abyss from which, if I glimpsed truth, I would not return. Presumptuous though this feeling was, it was extraordinarily real. I felt exhausted and went to lie between the moss-covered rocks that formed an armchair on the cliff overlooking the sun-burnished ocean. I fell asleep but after a while I woke again because some words were flooding my mind. Later I tried to write them down:

Only love emancipates man from his animal nature, so man's highest belief must surely be in God as original Love. Love at its finest concept, the root of all harmony, the height of all being, the Love that is Creation itself. There can be no higher concept of God, and we can perceive no more than this. Human love – the love of father, mother, friend, child, or love between man and woman – are only small subdivisions.

That was all. A fragment of an idea. But for a while longer I found myself thinking in ways I could not remember before.

Is not our ability to love spiritually our *only* God-like attribute? So surely only when we live lives that contribute to cosmic order and harmony, thus overcoming the insensitivities of raw nature, and of our own natures, are we expressing in the universe consciousness of that ideal we call God? If, in the ultimate sense, God exists far beyond the finite understanding of man, then living Love in this way is the only possible path to complete understanding, the only reconcilable bridge, the only certain way to align with the harmony of original Creation. It suddenly seemed clear to me that as we are the earth's dominant species, our responsibility lies not only to ourselves but to all other life on this planet, and this responsibility is not only inherent but utterly inescapable. Only through a regard for all life, by aligning spiritually with the harmonious forces in nature and from a height of feeling, transfiguring the inharmonious or callous in loving creative work, can we be at one with the source of true creativity and so be akin to what we call God.

I lay for a long time turning these ideas over and over in my mind. I thought then they would henceforth change my life, that wherever I went or whatever I did, I had found a code for living that made sense to me. I did not realise that afternoon that I would fail, as I have failed many times, through all-too-human weakness, to live up to them. But it seemed I had at least been given a hint, a key to a better life and I found myself looking at the world around me with new eyes.

Sight, stalk and 'shoot' …

I never considered myself a wildlife photographer and maybe some folks will say I was right. I always felt myself to be an observer, a mere student of nature, who stalked the lochs, forests and mountains taking detailed notes and then who wrote up those notes in as vital and telling a form as possible in my articles and books. Even during my three years in the wilds of western Canada I never owned a camera, so many of the photos in my Canadian wildlife book were taken by friends, while the ones I took, of grizzly bears and all other wildlife, were taken on cameras I briefly borrowed. Not until near the end of my first year in the wilds of the Scottish Highlands did I decide to actually buy a camera, and then really only to illustrate, and prove, the extraordinary things I was witnessing in the wild.

I started out with very basic equipment – and I ended up with basic equipment! First came a standard Pentax and then an Olympus 0M2 with a 300 mm lens. Not until my third year did I add a 640 mm Novoflex telephoto lens which had a pistol grip for fast focussing, and had only one piece of glass in its 2 ft 6 ins length. This was all still very basic gear yet it was with this combination I took the photos in this book.

No, I don't consider myself to be a professional nature photographer. I never bothered much with landscapes, or over shots of woodlands, marshes, sea scenes; nor the way frost forms on a leaf, misty dawns, spring's first leaves, flowers and the like – but I did make an exception for butterflies.

I mostly wanted to capture on film the most difficult and rare species – mammals that spot or scent you and flee fast on foot, or rare dramatic birds such as golden eagles which see you – and fly off! With the Novoflex lens, wildlife photography soon became for me an extension of the hunting instinct – I could spot a flying bird, a hunting mammal or, say, stags fighting, and whirl round, lift the lens, focus fast with the pistol grip in my left hand and press the camera button, the 'trigger', with my right forefinger. It was exactly the same movement one makes when 'rough shooting' with a shotgun, so I saw myself not so much as a photographer but as a hunter with a camera. The first five photos in this book were taken by this method, as were many of the others. I could sight, stalk and 'shoot' a rare, shy and secretive creature by using wilderness skills developed over years and end up with a beautiful picture of an animal or bird that remained free instead of it ending up as a 'trophy' and a dead body. And always I wanted to capture the sheer beauty of nature. Was it Keats or Yeats who wrote 'Truth is Beauty; and Beauty is Truth; and that's all ye need to know'?

I only managed to break into wildlife writing because of the *Reader's Digest*, after they accepted without any alterations (extremely rare for them) my first submitted story of how I brought up a young sparrowhawk. They commissioned several other wildlife stories over the next five years and their payments helped me to keep going with basic supplies in the wilds. I was even more grateful when their new book publishing company in America Reader's Digest Press published my first wildlife book – all about my years of adventures with grizzly bears, cougars, bald eagles and killer whales in Canada (*Alone in the Wilderness*). A UK publisher had refused to believe the story so I made a special costly trip back to Canada to take the photos to prove the book. The snag then was the American publisher refused to use the photos – saying my powers of description were so good they didn't need to use any pictures! I swore then I would never allow any wildlife book of mine to be published without photos to illustrate its truths, beauty, and increase the pleasure of the reader – and I never have.

I finally packed up wildlife stills photography for two main reasons. The first was when I saw a leading professional wildlife cameraman use his computer to remove on a photograph the jesses on a tame buzzard. I couldn't compete with that, nor did I want to. The second was when I took that fine naturalist and travel writer Brian Jackman on treks to see golden eagles for the half-page he was to write on me and my work for the *Sunday Times*. Obeying the inviolate wilderness law – if you want to see rare creatures leave your cameras at home – we saw five different eagles in twenty-four hours of daylight, something I'd never achieved when trekking on my own.

At the end of our third day we were on the highest mountain taking down my hide over an eagle's nest, when we were treated to an amazing spectacle. The mother eagle soared in with a ptarmigan in her talons and landed by her newly-flown eaglet. She opened up the carcass with her beak then flew off, to return a few minutes later with her mate. She hovered briefly over the ptarmigan, showing it to the male who then landed beside it, then she flew away. The male then taught the eaglet how to hunt, how to kill for he kept rising into the air, followed by the eaglet, then landing back on the carcass. This happened four times as we watched breathlessly. As soon as the eaglet got the idea and landed on the ptarmigan and began to feed, he flew off to join his mate.

We lowered our aching arms with the binoculars and Brian looked at me 'What a fantastic sight: What a life you lead'.
'Yes,' I replied with an ironic laugh.
'And I left the bloody camera at home! Imagine filming that.'
'You ought to get a movie camera.'
When I said I couldn't afford a film camera, Brian replied 'Ah, you can get a second hand Arriflex for around £250 to £300, an old one. They last for ever – you can knock nails in with them and they still work fine!'

Upshot? A few weeks later I did buy a 16 mm Arriflex camera – and for the last twenty five years have only filmed wildlife, making, so far, ten long rare, wildlife movies which I try to sell in VHS form to augment my meagre coffers.

I swiftly sold all my stills photographic gear to one of my readers – both cameras, the 300 mm lens, the fabulous Novoflex lens but not a tripod. I didn't sell him a tripod because I never had one! As I said, I was never a professional wildlife photographer. But I have a lot to thank Brian Jackman for.

How, and perhaps more pertinently, why did these ventures start? I'll go back to the beginning …

After years of successful journalism in many leading cities of Europe and America, I fled to the strangeness of western Canada to write what I hoped would be the Great Novel. The book failed but in those Pacific coastal wilds my big city hedonism had been exorcised, the love of nature I had discovered as a boy in Sussex had been reborn, and finally I trekked into the last remote fastnesses to watch grizzly bears, cougars, bald eagles and caribou in the wild. Then I became bewitched by a desire to try and live a wilderness life back in Britain. Perhaps obeying some deep ancestral calling – for my mother had been a Highlander – I indeed found it on the sea island of Eilean Shona, off the Inverness-shire coast. There, learning to live partly from the land and sea, had come my first close experiences with red deer, foxes, wildcats, sparrowhawks, herons, ravens, sea birds and seals. Yet those years served only to whet my appetite and my love for the rarest wildlife of the Highlands, still one of Europe's finest wild regions, had all the cravings of an unconsummated love affair.

Although my earlier romantic notions about nature had long been knocked out of me, I had become consumed by a passion to sink myself totally into one of Britain's last wild places, to live simply, close to the vital animal state myself, the full year round in an even wilder place of higher mountains, longer rivers and larger forests, amid greater remoteness, this time in a fresh water environment. Consequently, I moved to the wild cottage I came to call Wildernesse which was halfway up the north side of an eighteen-mile roadless loch. There was no electricity, telephone, TV, piped water, postal delivery, not even a road or track in. My only link with the outside world, to get supplies even in winter storms, was my small open boat. Only by doing this did I feel that by more persistent study, could I possibly understand the vast interplay of Highland nature, from strand of moss to massive oak, from tiny beetle and little wren to mighty stag and golden eagle, and perhaps communicate through my writings not only love for wildlife but the necessity of conserving, even enhancing, the inspiring natural world, for the sake of man himself. To communicate my own conviction that unless man redeems the heedless greed that has destroyed so much of that world he may yet destroy the very environment he needs for both physical and spiritual sustenance, and that he, once the brightest light of evolution, will end up its greatest failure. Pretentious aims they were of course but there was great adventure in it all too. Once, in mid-December a radio in the local store announced a Force 11 gale was 'imminent' in the area. As I'd be heading home in my open boat at least I would be going with it. It was getting dark so I took the risk. I had only covered half a mile when the storm hit the loch. Dark clouds rode up behind me on blue and violet palfreys, stinging my head with shrieking air. Deep in the watery troughs the prop laboured away but slowed down as the following wave pressed hard against the boat while she was held up by the back of the giant wave in front. Slowly she surged up it, then I had to hastily throttle down as she hurtled with a roar into the next trough, seeming about to go to the bottom. But, thank heaven she came out of it each time, her bow rising in a shower of spray, water pouring sideways off the semi-cabin and back into the boiling surface. Whirlpools of wind hit the loch like hammers on ice, skirling up spindrifts so that six-foot water spouts shot into the air with disconcerting suddenness ... I soon learned that the loch was my master, that it controlled my physical destiny, that on the long boat journeys to fetch supplies and post my writings it cradled my very life on its swelling deep, and that if I failed to treat it with care and respect it would fashion my end.

There was danger – but adventure too – up in the wild hills around my remote home. I remember the early treks, especially searching for golden eagles, when I'd go out with heavy camera pack and look at the first 500 ft ridges towering steeply above the cottage, knowing they had to be beaten first but were merely the prelude to higher slopes and ridges and beyond them more crests to peaks of 3,000 feet. And my heart would skip a beat as I knew what lay ahead. Within an hour I would be miles into a wilder landscape, forcing through deep tussocks where flowing grassy crowns disguised the treacherous gullies between them, skirting spongy bogs with floating beds of sphagnum mosses, floundering over black peat hags, negotiating steep rocky scree where a false step meant at least a bloody scraping fall, climbing rocky ravines carved over thousands of years by the burns, and pushing through jungles of high bracken that cut hands as painlessly as an anaesthetised surgeon's knife if I grabbed it to arrest a fall.

One early March trek I'd climbed to 1,500 feet, then down again and along the river of a steep glen for three miles, up to a 2,000-foot peak, back along the high saddle for a mile, then back down again to the river valley. I had seen nothing but primroses on a burn bank, a few hinds, a pair of flying ravens, a few molehills, and was then on the hard climb back up out of the glen. What a dreary slog it had become – one foot in front of the other, force the creaking painful knee straight again, then another step up, time after interminable time, zig-zagging yet again up the nearly sheer jagged ground. Miles of mostly staring down, every tussock, rock and slab of embedded granite beating its unseasonable heat back at me, my pack of camera, lenses, rainsuit, lunch, heavy on my back. My only consolation seemed to be if I fell now, going up, at least it would only be a matter of inches to the ground.

Still, all this and more had to be endured if I was to see wildlife at its finest in the mountains – the bachelor herds of red deer stags avoiding biting flies on the high plateaus; an eagle with wings tucked in dropping out of the sky a mile above, lit by the sun into a ball of gold, shooting upwards again after a brief opening of its wings, then repeating the deep undulating dives over two miles in a spectacular territorial display; a tawny wildcat slipping between boulders of a high rockfall; a distant fox beating long grasses with forepaws to shake out grasshoppers; a small pack of ptarmigan whirring over a ridge, snorting like little pigs at this rare intrusion into their lonely alpine world; or if I was to emerge finally upon the highest peak and survey far below a world of timelessness and mystery, where mountain followed mountain, and glen succeeded glen in a shimmering vista that seemed to have remained unchanged since time began, inspiring thoughts and insights that would never have come at my desk.

Even more needed to be endured for all the many years I studied golden eagles at their nests. In each season I had shivered through long nights on lonely cliff ledges, been drenched in constant rains, baked by the sun on long treks, knocked off my feet by raging burns, beleaguered by camera failures, scared of falling from the heights – I roped myself on when I could because when I woke up during the nights I didn't instantly know which side the drop was on. At the end of every season I swore I would never 'work eagles' again. But each autumn and winter I would witness new aspects of eagle life, realise there were still many things I wanted to know – and I also started actually filming them – so every spring back on would go my eagle boots. I spent a total of forty years working with eagles in the wild, culminating with filming nesting white-tailed sea eagles on my 76th birthday, but I intend to spend my next one, my 80th, filming eagles and only THEN will I finally hang up my eagle boots – I think.

They were lonely years from the human point of view, of course, and it was some time before I realised that only by creative work, in my case studying wildest nature, could I transform the agony of solitude. I think I succeeded – some of the time.

RED SQUIRRELS

The first creature I saw on my first boat trip to my most remote home, Wildernesse, was a red squirrel – which helped clinch the place in my mind as a good area to live. It was mainly to help them that I later planted many sweet chestnut trees. I watched one giving the hazel bushes a real working over as it hunted for nuts. The popular phrase 'forest sprite' seemed inapt because, for its size, it had a burly powerful body, seemed tireless and to be nearly all muscle. Its big eyes bulging with intent, it grabbed a branch with one hand, pulled it down to see if there were any nuts there, then let it go. Sometimes it thrust the branch away with an aggressive push as if to help it on its fidgety way. As it jumped from one to another I saw that it kicked against already rising branches to give it its upward leap more impetus, just as it kicked against the down-moving branches to reach one below more quickly. It worked with blinding speed, was baffling to watch, and very hard to photograph. It was a full year before I got these sunlit shots when they were momentarily still enough.

WHOOPER SWANS

In the deserted lakes of the vast tundra the female whooper swan incubates her three to five creamy-white to bluish eggs, which hatch exceptionally quickly for their size – sometimes in less than thirty five days, up to nine days faster than the golden eagle. The cygnets can fly when they are just over eight weeks old. Then all the birds concentrate on feeding, building stamina and strength for the great southerly flight back to their winter dormitories in Britain and Ireland, where about two thousand of them stay on the Scottish lochs.

Many a time in late October or early November have I been enthralled while in my boat to see a flock winging in from the far north. Sometimes they pass so close I can hear their great wings whistling like wind harps and the music of their voices as they communicate with each other with melodic 'ungh' and 'angha' calls. Often they look tired, and well they might after their 500-mile non-stop journey maintaining speeds of around fifty miles an hour. One by one they widely extend their dark webbed feet, like the landing gear of planes, and with winnowing feathery back strokes of their wings, sloosh down into the brassy bright surface of the loch. Instantly each bird stretches its graceful long neck and beak deep into the water – how good it must feel to take a drink and rest at last after so heroic a flight, after their long night's journey into day.

Every autumn as the whoopers come winging in, sometimes shining like silver ghosts in the dawn light before the sun rises beyond the hills, there is a great sense of continuity, of permanence, about the joy I feel at seeing the great white angels of the loch back again.

Whoopers are not strictly 'colony' birds, though they form loose small feeding flocks in winter because they know there is safety in numbers when they feed on water plants, insects, and graze on marshy waterside pastures. If one bird spots a pair of predatory foxes, or a frisky dog, its sudden calling and flying up warns the others, and the scattering of the flock makes it harder for a single victim to be concentrated upon. They also 'talk' to each other when grazing, making soft 'owoo' and 'whooau' sounds, and each swan spaces itself from its fellows so it has plenty of room to look around, feed and fly up without collision should there be an alarm.

Only very rarely do whooper swans nest on Scottish lochs. They cannot breed successfully until four or five years old, and as they live up to twenty years or more they also spend some of their last years without breeding. So most of the few whoopers still seen in the Highlands in summer are non breeders which have not made the long northerly fight, being either too young or too old.

Two whooper swans, freshly back from their 500-mile flight from their nesting areas in Iceland, are lit up by the late October sun as they take off from the river that drains their winter loch.

After underwater fishing, a cormorant seems to pose like a ballerina
as it holds its wings wide open to dry in the sun-filled breeze.

A lapwing flies round the human intruder making strident calls, trying to distract attention from her new hatched chicks in their nest on the ground.

REDWINGS

In early October flocks of redwings, up to two hundred strong, come winging in from Scandinavia. They fill the woods with sweet 'quip quip' calls for two or three days, raid the beech mast, hover with bright flashes of their red underwing patches to strip the rowans of berries and then, stomachs full, depart for the rich pickings of the farmlands to the west before continuing southwards. Powerful fliers for small birds, they seldom land for a rest on ships or oil rigs on their 400-mile flight over the North Sea, and after a day's rest they easily outmanoeuvre the resident thrushes and blackbirds when they hunt for snails, worms, beetles and caterpillars.

Redwings are increasingly liking Scotland, began nesting there in 1953 and today there can be upwards of sixty breeding pairs a year. Once I was lucky enough get a fine photo of one hovering, a bright berry in its beak, at ninety yards by swinging my 2 ft 6 ins telephoto lens onto it in a 'rough shooting' method.

A redwing thrush hovers briefly to snatch an autumn berry from a rowan tree. This is a fine example of the kind of 'lucky' photo when I 'rough shoot' with the fast pistol-grip focussing of my 640 mm lens.

One lonely Christmas in the wild I saw a titchy wren searching through cold, snowy bracken fronds for food and like King Alfred with the spider, I gained inspiration from its tenacity and courage.

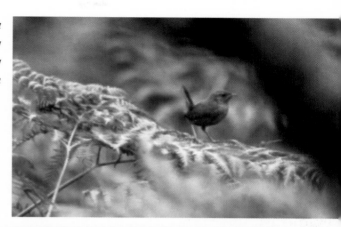

Whenever I lived in the wilds, even many miles from civilisation, I always was glad to have robins around my home, a bird I regard as bold rather than 'tame'. Robins will battle each other more fiercely for territories than other birds.

The huge tom wildcat, nearly four feet long, mounted a big slab of rock, then stopped and turned round. It glared towards me with magnificent green-gold eyes, its huge thick striped tail resting on the ground. To photograph a pure wildcat actually in the wild is extremely rare but after a freezing long predawn wait I had almost miraculous luck.

WILDCATS

At the store a friend told me he had seen a huge wildcat early that very morning in the fields above the pier where I left my boat.

It seemed a forlorn hope for few humans have ever photographed a wildcat in the wild. Even so I prowled around below a huge rockslide under some towering cliffs in which ravens were nesting and there, in a marshy patch among the winter-battered old grasses, I found two unmistakeable four-toed tracks of a cat, too circular for a fox and too large for a wandering domestic cat … I hid at the edge of a small wood downwind of the area and watched the courting ravens but they were too far for a photo, and it was now too dark anyway.

Only then did I see the animal in front of me, a mere 30 yards away. It looked almost as big as a roe deer, its legs hidden between the deep grassy tussocks. A heavy, thick-bodied creature with a dark tawny-grey coat, surely too large for any cat, was slipping along through some patches of heather. It paused, lifted its head and then I saw the short muzzle, the broadly spaced pointed ears. It was a wildcat, a huge tom, I judged, and it kept low as it headed for some small willow bushes growing in a bog, beyond which were open fields where rabbits had their burrows. It was hunting, and now and again it paused to sniff the air, as if stalking as much by scent as by sight.

Despite the gathering dusk, I tried to take a photo, but the wildcat heard the shutter's click, turned but too briefly for me to take another, and slipped away like a ghost. I stayed unmoving for half an hour in the increasing cold, knowing that any movement would give away my exact position. I didn't see it again.

I camped in the Land Rover at the pier overnight and rose in the early twilight and, without bothering with breakfast, stole through the woods and hid myself overlooking the open boggy patch, ready for a long cold wait. As the light improved

I heard a cock chaffinch give its tripping song. Then a pair of tawny owls began calling to each other behind me in the woods.

I had waited about forty freezing minutes before I caught a brief glimpse of the wildcat. It appeared between two large tussocks turned south and vanished. I hadn't moved. Nor did I try to take a picture for it was still too dark and there was no point scaring it. I waited another five minutes, ten, half an hour. Suddenly I saw it again, coming back!

Quivering with excitement and cold, I watched, fascinated, as it stalked along, its head low but moving up and down slightly with every second stride. Occasionally it stopped to peer about and sniff the air, with one paw upraised. It was indeed a large animal and my heart pounded. Slowly I checked the meter switch. At a thirtieth of a second the needle barely quivered. Treading carefully and yet somehow ponderously, the wildcat came slowly nearer, raced across the little one-track road in a crouching run, as a soldier does when afraid of air attack, then sneaked along through the grass and heather again.

As it reached the open area before me I tried a shot. Even at that distance it heard the click. I cursed silently. But it moved on, mounted a big slab of rock, then stopped and turned round. Perfecto Click! It was glaring straight towards me, with magnificent green-gold eyes, its huge thick striped tail resting on the ground. Risk a 60th. Click. Then it disappeared over a grassy ridge and into the rocky cairns of the slide.

It was the kind of miraculous luck that only comes to a beginner. Later, I used the photo to measure the wildcat's image over the ground – that big tom must have been nearly four feet long. Knowing it would be useless to stalk such a wary keen-sensed creature, I put the camera and lens into their plastic bags in my pack and boated back to the croft with yesterday's supplies.

Two magnificient specimens of pure wildcat, female and male, living in a large natural enclosure. There are believed to be less than 500 pure wildcats left in the Scottish Highlands, due to many years of interbreeding with feral cats.

At my remote home, which I could only reach by boat, I bred wildcats and re-leased a total of eight back to the wild. This is the father of the kittens, ferocious 16 lb Sylvesturr who usually greeted me with a foot stamp and a loud spit. I always knew where I stood with him – total, inviolate hatred.

Female wildcat, Cleo, takes her first two-month old kittens for an airing outside their den.

The first wildcat family went free at the end of July and I used my gentle giant German Shepherd Moobli to track them, putting them up trees so I could check their condition.

At six months old wildcat kittens can be quite fierce when playing.

The male wildcat kitten showed much of his father's ferocity and distrust of humans even at only nine and a half weeks old.

And he hadn't lost it at six months old.

With heathlands becoming more scarce down south due to intensive farming, the Scottish Highlands have become cuckoos' main stronghold. Once a cuckoo starts to lay she has an egg to deposit roughly once every two days, and she uses isolated branches looking for meadow pipits' nests and has to memorise up to a dozen nests. This method saves her having to make laborious flying searches. Cuckoos' favourite food are large hairy caterpillars, like those of the large eggar moths, and I noticed they often glide against the wind into prey so they don't have to beat their wings hard and startle their prey off its perch by a noisy arrival.

On a sunny day a beautiful female kestrel landed below my open window. My camera, set up for wild pine marten at night, just had to be tipped slightly to focus on her.

A male kestrel devours a mouse held in his talons which he had caught on the forest floor below his nests.

Black and yellow-ringed hawker dragonflies are much easier to approach when they are mating, being occupied by more vital activities.

DRAGONFLIES

I liked to watch a great black and blue striped aeshna dragonfly hunting in the sun. It hawked about, swooping with contemptuous ease to catch flies and gnats in the scoop formed from its massive jaws and thick black legs. Sometimes it came to investigate my face, hovering with rattling wings and treating me to the frightful primeval stare of a pair of bulging multi-lensed eyes that blazed like twin mirrors with a metallic sheen. Then it would spot some worthy prey, like a big buzzing bluebottle, sweep up like a falcon at a finch and snatch it from the air.

Dragonflies have long been my favourite insects for it was they who helped start my love affair with nature. As a city boy of twelve on his first country holiday I discovered a little wild pond in the woods, and above it floated these incredible creatures of darting fire. As they hawked over the reeds, snatching insects on the wing, they had 'minds' of their own, clearly knew exactly what they were doing. Clearly, they were the dashing Red Barons of the insect world. Dragonflies are a miracle of evolution and have been hunting this way for 340 million years. Even the aeshnas we see today are Britain's oldest flying predators and were hawking the skies 150 million years ago, long before the first dinosaurs appeared.

Their eyes are among the most efficient in creation, and contain thousands of lenses. Few insects can see more than six feet in front of them, but if just one of a dragonfly's hexagonal lenses perceives a fast movement up to forty feet away, its lighting reflexes and aerobatic skills allow it to investigate immediately, make a capture – or flee.

It is a shame that dragonflies are in decline, due to many of their breeding ponds have being polluted, allowed to silt up or filled in for development purposes, for these magnificent insects are immensely useful to man. Both as a larval nymph in the water and as a flying adult, one dragonfly kills thousands of mosquitoes, midges, flies and wasps in its lifetime. When it hovers around farm animals – or you – it is not about to sting as was once believed (it has no sting) but to catch pests like botflies whose larvae invade the animals' noses and stomachs, or greenbottles whose maggots feed on any injured flesh.

I watched a male dragonfly put his mating technique into action – it left much to be desired from the romantic view but it was stunningly effective. When a browner female came winging round from behind a hazel bush, he shot upwards at great speed, hit into her with an audible clash, then seized her neck with the special anal claspers at the end of his 3 ½ inch body. Down they went, their wings buzzing noisily like a clockwork train left running in the grass. She seemed totally submissive to his headstrong desire and within a minute both flew back into the air, their wingbeats sychronising, and landed on a bracken fern where she curled her tail up under his body and mated. For several more minutes they flew round the area in tandem, then he let her go. I watched her fly towards the loch's edge where she would lay her eggs on a water plant.

Towards the end of March the common gulls come winging up the loch like tiny white angels to take over again their nesting area on the rocky islet near my remote home. Once some of them realised I was putting out scraps, the bolder ones would often land on my chimney pot and wait for the extra tidbits.

A large boar badger
emerges from his sett
in a beech wood.

Badgers are common in the Highlands, preferring to dig their setts in woodlands but here they often have to use the open hills. Early breeders, they line their nests with molinia and long dry grasses dragged in backwards by both front feet. Most mating takes place in February to May, sometimes taking up to fifteen minutes a time. Also a bit like humans they enjoy sexual activity and can mate again up to October. The original blastocyst (fertilised embryo) persists so no more fertilisation takes place from later intercourse. If man could learn that trick, our overpopulation problems could be solved! After finding an old sheep carcass that had been neatly flensed, as if by a big cat like a cougar, the skin and fur rolled back cleanly from the meat, my German Shepherd tracker dog Moobli tracked the animals' scents up to a big sett at 600 feet. Rows of deep toilet pits were filled with loose oily black droppings, proving that the badgers had stuffed themselves with the pure meat, also proving they readily eat carrion. I left them to sleep it off for three days, then went back with camera, flash gun and tripod – and got great shots of the boar coming out to waddle off to feed – big fellow he was too, weighing about 30 lbs. And in very fine shape indeed, his coat glossy after his nourishing feeds.

I was surprised one late June to find a badger romping about on the open hill above my cottage in full daylight. When it hesitated after first getting my scent, I could press the camera button.

When a small female badger began coming to the foods I set out at night, I saw she was increasingly looking weak and shaky on her feet. When I managed to catch her in a box-cage live trap I'd invented, I found she had deep wounds in her neck which were festooned with maggots. I had to treat her. When, after much soothing talk, I managed to lift her out wearing thick gloves her head whirled round and she bit hard. I could feel the power of her jaws but strangely she just took hold of my fingers and didn't bite with full power; as if she was indicating she had me now and if I hurt her she would bite really hard. She didn't like having a bath in my kitchen sink but I avoided her snaps at my gloves and I managed to clean her wounds and treat them with antibiotic cream. She soon settled down, sleeping in a hay-filled den box and having free run of the kitchen. Inside two weeks after a spell in the old wildcat pens she went back to the wild. I was most gratified when she again started coming back at night for the foods I set out.

I did not realise that badgers, heftily-built animals, could climb like monkeys until I set out raisins and currants and nuts in the crevices of this old fallen tree.

One May morning I was astonished when I was able to sneak up on the area's largest dog fox when he was feeding avidly from a deer calf carcass at the top of my west wood. He looked up suspiciously once but did not see me.

Full of meat, his belly slightly distended, he plodded back through the tussocks towards his den.

A large vixen came to investigate young foxes I was looking after.

She was most interested in this one.

All the young foxes had been caught by the foot in gin traps. But they swiftly recovered and I had to put them on ropes and collars so they couldn't escape when not yet able to look after themselves in the wild. They often had playful mock battles, making high yickering squeaks, like big mice.

When the boisterous young vixen wanted to play with the reluctant shyer one, she just hauled her nearer by the rope!

When alone, they were always on the alert, looking out for danger.

An alert, suspicious fox club peering through bracken.

The colourful cock chaffinches were bossy, often driving the hens off food on the bird table. But they took good care of their chicks. Here in late July one is about to feed a soliciting chick, which is trembling its wings and making little chirruping sounds.

LONG-TAILED TITS

Sometimes the air is filled with high ringing 'si si sis' as a party of long tailed tits, winter flocking with coal and blue tits, flit through the trees around me. With their long three-inch tails, and tiny bodies even smaller than wrens', they look like flying crochets escaped from nature's music sheet.

BULLFINCHES

In early spring I see with a mixture of delight and regret some flashing white lights among the early creamy blossoms on my fruit trees and hear faint 'dui' calls. The lovely, cussed, bullfinch tribes are back again, devastating the buds of my future crops and the 'lights' are the pure white rumps of the rosy-breasted males. All summer, autumn and winter I see them not at all but come the first hint of spring back they come. Clearly because mine are the only fruit trees in twelve miles of lochside, they remember where they are and know the time to come.

Now they are hard at work, as acrobatic as tiny parrots, twisting and twirling and scattering blossom petals. As I walk over, two of the males, dark eyes hidden in their black stormtrooper-helmeted heads, fly up from a rainwater runnel where they have been slaking their thirst. Sometimes I clap my hands to scare them off for a while, so they might get the idea to leave a few buds but mostly I don't. I don't mind too much as I always have enough fruit left for my own needs and I now know that spring is really on its way.

For a bird that is perhaps nature's most perfect killing machine, I often feel the peregrine lets itself down sometimes, because whenever a human goes near a nest with eggs or chicks the birds kick up a terrible racket, with screaming 'raich raich' calls and whirling round above you, thus actually showing you the nest. Even so although she is only eighteen inches long, the peregrine falcon is the climax of evolutionary perfection. Here is my description of one hunting on a common gulls nesting islet:

'Her slaty-blue back reflected the bright azure of the sky, her creamy narrow-barred chest feathers were held tight to her body, and the black moustaches below her steely-blue hooked beak gave a solemn cast to her hunter's face. Now, from over half a mile away, she selected her victim and launched herself from the crest. A few strong beats and she was up into the full vortex of the wind. She angled her wings back and began to move … I saw her arcing across the sky like a meteor. Down, down, down she stooped across the blue curving firmament of the sky at incredible speed, then was lost to sight behind a small wood. I dashed down to get a clear view but was too late, for all I saw was her beating away to the east with a light brown feathery bundle in her talons – a fledged gull chick which could never have known what hit it. I felt breathless, amazed. It was all over in a moment, a flash of time. The gulls, who mobbed and harrassed any crow or buzzard that passed by, could never have seen her coming, or if they did, had no time to do anything about it. Now they flew distractedly, with indignant shrieks of fear and frustration, impotent against nature's lightning slayer.

'To see the hunting flight of the peregrine falcon, which can snap off a pigeon's head with just one strike, is to re-evaluate all of nature, for it is a primeval god.'

A peregrine chick calls to its mother who is flying overhead.

I was astonished after a long hike over open unpromising hills to come upon three well-fed peregrine chicks in an eyrie in a small cleft only fifteen feet above the ground. Their ledge was thick with a carpet of pigeons' remains and feathers

PEREGRINE FALCON

On the high crag I watched her preening her breast feathers, stretching one dark wing and one foot down towards the ground and lifting both bent wings high above her head in 'Hottentot' stretches. What a superb creature she was, smart black and blue-grey wings, the lovely soft plumage of her cream and navy-blue-barred chest looking pinkish in the direct sunlight, great hunter face so solemn with its dark moustaches, all her movements wonderful. Like the eagle, here was a creature beyond man, living in her own world, resting and flying when she felt like it, killing when she was hungry or needed to feed her young; no attitudes, no intellectual pretension, glorying only in being alive.

In the late 1930s it was estimated there were 650 pairs of peregrines nesting in Britain, despite harrassment by some keepers and egg collectors. They were heavily shot and persecuted during World War Two as they were a threat to carrier pigeons carrying vital messages when radio silence was essential. Their numbers began to recover but in the early 1960s they were decimated by agricultural pesticides getting into the bodies of their prey, usually flying birds, causing sterility and thin-shelled eggs which broke in the nest. After scientific surveys the most lethal pesticides were banned in 1974. Numbers began to rise again, despite continued illegal taking of eggs and chicks, and it is heartening to know that today Britain's peregrine populations exceed even their pre-war populations, estimated at over 2,000 individuals.

WILDERNESS PHILOSOPHY

Living alone in the wilds can be a lonely business. It was some years before I realised that only through creative work could I transform the agony of loneliness into the glory of solitude.

Three hungry fully-fledged peregrine chicks call loudly when they see a parent coming in with prey. They flew a week later after spending some days perched on various ledges around the nest.

Three goshawk chicks in their larch tree nest which is characteristically in a dark wood, and usually hard to photograph or film. Once extinct in the UK there are now around 400 pairs, though they suffer from egg and chick thieves. They prefer larch for their nests as the needle-filled sprays are knotted and hold together well. Ounce for ounce, the goshawk is the most powerful British bird of prey and can bring down a flying pheasant.

When looking for fish on which to dive, ospreys are less afraid of humans than most large birds of prey, and with their five-foot wing spans are an inspiring sight.

Two adult ospreys in their flat tree-top nest. Extinct at the turn of the last century, the last pair nesting in 1916, the birds were regular migrants from Africa to Scandinavia and began recolonising Scotland in the 1950s. A fabulous and unique protection and viewing scheme was started at Loch Garten by the RSPB and from that first pair, the UK population has increased to over 200 pairs. By 2005 they began recolonising England and Wales and there are now nine sites where we can watch them. Some 300,000 people visit these sites each year, spending £3.5 million in surrounding areas, so supporting local employment.

When seen fishing it is easy to see herons as loners but I've seen them hunting frogs in a field as a team, and have witnessed their communal 'dancing' grounds, with as many as twenty nine herons performing a sort of truncated gavotte. This is said to stimulate their social instincts and sex hormones before selecting mates and breeding.

A young heron trying to catch fish in a shallow burn. I have seen adult herons up to their 'hips' in sea water perform a slow side to side waltz, and it was easy to understand why the mediaevals believed they secrete special oil from their feet to attract fish! Herons suffer in severe winters and have sometimes been found dead with water frozen round their legs.

A heron I had put back in its nest after falling out in a storm often used my boat bay for fishing. Here, it flies off at dusk.

A most extraordinary bird is the plump seven-inch long dipper. It is a familiar sight in the north and west as it perches on rocks in rushing streams and bobs its tail and dips its bright white chest up and down like a small torch in the dark surroundings. It can walk under water in flowing streams by angling its back so the water presses it down as it searches for water larvae, nymphs and small fish like minnows. It can walk under still water by clinging to stones with its exceptionally strong feet. It can dive and 'swim' under water using its wings as paddles and because of the air bubbles trapped in its plumage it looks like a giant blob of mercury moving along. I have been surprised when looking at tranquil waters to witness a dipper shoot to the surface and without a pause rise into the air with the ease of a miniature Polaris missile. I can think of no other water bird that can perform all these feats.

A black-throated diver hesitates in the water, making sure the coast is clear, before making her way to her nest and two eggs, which are always close to the water's edge.

BLACK-THROATED DIVERS

No other creatures so embody the wild spirit of the Highland lochs than the magnificent black-throated divers. Extremely rare – there are less than 150 breeding pairs so they are three times more rare than golden eagles – they are very wary, hard to study yet are immensely fascinating. Heavily built and some 28 inches long, they look like arrows of twanging steel when flying high on their short but powerful wings. They can dive to great depths, travel a quarter of a mile underwater, outswim their fishy prey, sink low when paddling along by emptying their air sacs, adapt to both salt and fresh water, and are extremely solicitous when taking care of their young. Their magnificent summer plumage with its rich blend of light greys, blue greys, purples, blacks, creamy underparts, sooty throat patches and snowy wing bars, must be the most spectacular of all water birds.

For a long time it was believed that divers were unable to walk because their legs, used mainly for ultra-efficient underwater swimming, are set too far back. But here I watched a diver reach the shore, put her beak to the ground, hauls herself upright in this fashion, then start to WALK up the slight slope to her nest. Click! And I had a perfect shot of the seemingly impossible – a black-throated diver walking.

he sun came up to light up such a magnificent view I truly felt that somehow I had entered paradise. The diver at motionless on her eggs, her bright orange eye unblinking, her startling plumage so perfect she looked unreal, ke a glazed precious ornament. Wavy black and white lines around and below the sooty black throat patch merged oftly into the pinky-cream of the belly feathers. Symmetrical black and white griddles, shimmering like moonlight n ruffled waters, adorn the blue-black wings and back. The sun's rays burnished the shoulders into greeny gold ighlights, and round white spots, all of different sizes, freckled the neat round edges of the outer wing feathers. Two ocks, blazing with diamonds of sparkling mica chips, led the eyes into a profusion of 'kingcup' marsh marigolds ehind the diver and their broad bright yellow flowers swayed iridescently in the light breeze, shining the early light ack to the sun.

This diver lost her first eggs to flash floods but re-laid in a new nest in late June.

A rare sight – a pair of divers swimming with their newly hatched two chicks. Their breeding success can be as low as 5% in some harsher seasons. Being close to the water their nests can be wrecked by flash floods after heavy rains cause lochs to rise. They also suffer from fishermen in boats going, often unwittingly, too close to their nests, the same with canoeists. They also suffer from predation by foxes and, yes, even otters. And I have known wildcats to swim from the mainland to take the eggs.

A wild mallard duck with her brood of young ducklings. I was lucky enough to get this photo because while mallards in towns like Hawick will stumble over your feet if you feed them, in the wild they are very wary and will take off after spying a human a quarter mile away.

EIDER DUCKS

There were small mating flocks of eider ducks out in the sea, the males sireing their mates with soft drawn-out 'awhoo' calls, a sweet music to usher in the warmer days of spring. Through my binoculars I saw one resplendent black and white drake swim round a dowdier brown female like a hefty little tugboat, tossing his massive wedge-shaped beak skywards, as if he were gulping. He really was a solid barge of a duck, decked out in superb evening dress, his black jacket a startling contrast to his white back and snowy velvet cheeks beneath his black-capped head. On his white breast was a patch of delicate peach, and overlaying each wing were long white plumes, fine enough to grace the hat of the Laughing Cavalier.

In the nesting season, when the females are incubating eggs, the eider duck drakes form seaside social gatherings, like an avian working mens' club.

With his chestnut breast, long beak and double spiky crests on his bottle-green head, the male red breasted merganser looks like a duck masquerading as Woody Woodpecker. Keepers dislike mergansers as they take young trout and salmon fry, but they take a lot of eels and baby pike too.

For years, otters were my 'bete noire', creatures I wanted to capture with my lens but always eluded me. My one d[...] of success on the seashore was after a whole sheet of otter photos sank into the loch when my boat went down in[...] storm. It was eight years until I saw this otter emerge from the sea with a crab in its mouth. After eating the crab[...] treated the seaweed as a bed, rolling over on its back and wriggling its body and thick tail from side to side. It the[...] turned the right way up and used the weed as a whisker and mouth cleaner, wiping first one side of its jaws and hea[...] and then the other, like a human uses a towel.

An otter leaving a dropping known as a 'spreint', on a rock on the water line. Otters leave these spreints for three main reasons – to help meet others of their kind in heat, for a female with young to warn other otters to stay out of her preferred hunting area, and for males to inform other males of their status, in size and maturity, so that actual fighting is rare as the juniors tend to avoid the seniors. Otters were legally protected in England and Wales in 1978 but not until 1981 in Scotland. This was long overdue as the Highlands are Britain's main reservoir of the animals.

An otter rolling on its back in the grass.

I had just crossed the burn, at the start of a trek on April 3rd, when I saw a roebuck ahead, the largest I'd seen so f
but he was grazing, his head too low to be seen. Having cast last year's antlers in early December, his new ones we
just three-quarters grown and still covered in greeny-brown velvet, like little mossy branches. But the light was to
poor for a correct exposure. 'Come on sun' I whispered then soon wished I hadn't made the wish for at the same tin
as his head came up, the clouds rolled by, and the sun gleamed down and the shadows of the slim trunks of a haz
bush above him showed up all over his coat, like prison bars. Roe deer have a white rump patch and when alarme
its hairs can be erected to form an alarm 'powder puff'. Roes are not popular in young forests for apart from chasir
each other, barking and anointing they fray vegetation with their antlers when acquiring or defending territori
from April to August.

ROE DEER

I carried on through the steep oak and birch woods, and had just located my twentieth badgers' sett below the tangled branches of a fallen tree, when I saw something reddish ahead. It was a sprightly little roebuck, superb in his summer coat, all lit up by dappled light in a green dell. I looked away, slowly removed my pack, fitted long lens onto camera and darned if he didn't stay there while I clicked off three fine photos before he galloped upwards to the north-east like a great red hare.

WILDERNESS PHILOSOPHY

There are no benefits or national health systems in the kingdoms of the wild. The code of the wild is harsh, but efficient – early death to the unfit, the unwary or the foolish, so they don't pass on their genes.

In late May I trekked to investigate an old oak snag which stood alone in bare terrain near a river and was surprised to find two semi-fledged tawny owlets blinking sleepily in a nest hollow. They showed little alarm, just clopping their beaks and they looked like little cowled monks.

A male tawny owl with mouse in beak.

I found out a lot about tawny owls when I looked after a small male that had been injured on the Highland roads. When I held out water in tins he quibbled his beak in it, lifted his head up to let the drops go down his throat. If I held out a red container he just nibbled at its edge but did not drink. He clearly thought the red was meat. He could definitely taste, preferring kidney, beef, liver in that order. If I gave him more after he'd eaten enough, he just held it in his beak, nibbled a few times, then dropped it. If I offered him bread he held it in one foot, tugged bits off with his beak, appeared to taste them with his tongue, then tossed them up into the air. But he kept pecking at the bread as if hoping to find meat beneath. He always kept his beak clean, wiping his beak on left and right sides on his hazel perch, like a man stropping a razor. He always ate the head of mice first, swallowing the skull and brains before tugging meat and fur from the rest of the body, always holding prey in his left foot. Yet when he scratched an itch on his head he always did it with one amazingly accurate talon on his right foot. He often flew into the study and landed on my shoulder as I sat typing at my desk, and he would nibble gently up and down on my ear, a definite expression of affection. He loved being tickled under the chin, stretching himself up to full height, his eyes half closed blissfully. He finally went free in the woods but sometimes returned, and I'd see him gazing down at me with what seemed smiles.

A male tawny in the woods, holding his favourite 'lollipop', a woodmouse.

I also looked after a beautiful young female tawny who insisted on perching on one of my sets of stag antlers. If not really hungry she would hold the mouse in her beak for several minutes while gazing rapturously into space, as if anticipating the easy meal ahead.

She often flew round the kitchen showing her beautiful wings before landing on her favourite perch.

Tree creepers work spirally up the trunks of trees, searching every cranny with sharp eyes for tiny insects but are hard to photograph as they are quite secretive. Once one landed on a larch tree right next to me and I hastily took this photo. Too hastily, for it was the last frame of a film and seconds later the tree creeper pulled a long squirming white grub from the bark – which would have been a better pictured.

It is usually hard to spot tawny owls in the wild because they slightly change their body shape and perch close to a trunk, trying to look like part of it.

A barn owl soars into her nest in the chimney stack of an old farmhouse with her long legs extended for landing, and a woodmouse in her beak for her chicks.

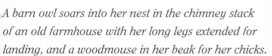

When I lived in a remote farmhouse in a hundred square miles forest in the Borders, I decided to try and redress the balance in my area. I obtained these six young barn owls from the Barn Owl Trust in Devon (before government licences were needed to keep the species) and reared them in my byre to maturity. I fed them on culled dead day-old chicks from a big local hatchery. Eventually, I established three pairs in a radius of three miles from my farmhouse. They all bred with varying success for the next two years then I sold my home. I later found out that the third pair had been killed by goshawks. Sad, but that is nature – one rare predator killing another.

The first pair to fly showed temporary interest in a plastic barrel I tied up a lodgepole pine.

barn owl perched on a rafter in an old barn. Barn owls prefer to roost in roofed buildings as their soft flight feathers, vital for silent hunting flight, are more prone to become waterlogged in the rain than other birds of prey. The species has been declining for fifty years, first from gamekeeper persecution, in the 1960s from pesticides building up in the bodies of prey, and finally from the modernisation of old barns and buildings, often into new homes for humans. It is believed there are now less than 15,000 barn owls left in all the UK, which is unfortunate, especially to farmers and small holders, as a pair of barn owls can kill 3,000 small rodents a year, including rats.

After they'd flown my barn owls often came at dusk and night to dead day-old chicks I set out on a bird table. I tacked the chicks to the table so the owls had to stay a few seconds tugging them free, giving me time to take photos.

Barn owls have acute hearing, in fact they hunt their prey rustling in the grasses more by sound than by sight. Even when I took photos from inside the study window they still heard the click of the shutter.

was delighted when a pair of colourful
jays came to the bird table. I agree with
the great naturalist W.H. Hudson who
called them 'Britain's bird of paradise'.

was even happier when a beautiful female kestrel began coming to the bird table and I had to up my quota of day-
ld chicks. She came for two years but was killed by a goshawk in the second winter, and I found her remains on one
f the hawk's plucking posts, a tree stump.

Once a female sparrowhawk came to the table, saw no chicks were left, and used it as a perch to crouch down and launch herself at a chaffinch.

Although I saw the strike I was inside the study and could not see where she ate the bird. But she returned to the bird table with the chaffinch now inside her, giving a real 'podgy' look.

In the same barn where the owls lived, a pair of swallows nested successfully.

SPARROWHAWKS

The dashing cavaliers of woodland glades and gardens, sparrowhawks were common for centuries but declined heavily from the mid 1960s as they fed on farmland birds which contained agricultural poisons such as DDT, which built up in their bodies and caused long-term poisoning and thin egg shells so there were many breeding failures. They were also persecuted by gamekeepers for predating on game bird chicks. When many pesticides were banned, and the hawks were given legal protection in 1966, numbers built up again and they spread back to many of their old areas. There are estimated to be well over 4,000 pairs in the UK today.

Many readers have written to me that they are ambivalent about admiring the fast-flying sparrowhawk when they see it taking tits and finches from their bird tables but the truth is not that predation by the hawk controls or limits the numbers of small birds. Quite the opposite; it is the numbers and availability of the small birds that control the hawks' numbers. More small birds are killed by cats, cars or flying into windows, than by sparrowhawks. The increasingly common ring or collared doves, absent from the UK fifty years ago, are an important modern source of prey.

A young long-seared owl chick on the old crow's nest in which it had been reared. Oddly, it was only 15 feet up, above a public footpath. The adults' ear tufts have nothing to do with hearing, being just longer head feathers. This owl's real ears are placed on the sides of its head so one ear is higher than the other. This gives a time lag between the same sound wave reaching each ear, enabling the owl to locate the precise position of its live prey. Fourteen inches long, long-eared owls have been known to kill birds as large as jays and crows among their usual diet of rats, mice, voles, shrews and some small birds. Its low mournful hoot is one of the ghostlier sounds of the woodland night.

WOODLAND SPRING

In the clearings the first grasses are greening the earth. Violets appear almost apologetically, as if modestly selecting careful places. The dark rosettes of bluebell leaves begin to starfish the ground, and by mid April the swellings at the heads of the thick stems begin to break open. Soon the woods are carpeted in a moving mosaic of yellows, greens, violets and blues, the white petals of wood sorrel drooping disconsolately if it rains. All the flowers bask in the springtime sun before the trees grow their leafy canopies and cast a dense shade. Slowly the bluebells take over so the clearings between the trunks and the side meadow are clouded in a blue so deep and rich it appears to herald the colour of the summer skies to come.

By mid April too, far ahead of other trees, the wild cherries are covered with white blossoms. Now the well-fuzzed larches are growing crimson female flowers, and along the lochshore pussy willows are silvering the bushes with shimmering light. The rowans are next, sending out tight inward-folding spears of silky silvery green plumes and from a few yards away they look like swords pointing to heaven. Close rivals are the hazels which dangle tiny sheaves from the ends of myriad twigs, like hankies being waved to a Queen. In late April long slender buds on the zig-zag twigs of the beeches burst open and pale green leaves unfold, tiny fans fringed with gossamer. On a breezy day thousands of their light brown covering scales fall like gentle rain.

A rare pine marten foraging for food. It took four years from first sighting of the marten in the woods round my remote loch-side home to get him tame enough to come to me for food.

I made a complicated log run and bird table complex on which to feed the birds and the marten, who later brought his mate and families along too. Pine martens date from the Eocene period. They survived the last Ice Age and their remains have been found in forty million years old deposits. When much of Scotland was covered with ancient Caledonian pine forests, and there were far more woods in England, Wales and Ireland than there are today, they were both common and widespread. For centuries, however, they were highly prized for their fur and were heavily trapped. They were also regarded as vermin and were trapped and shot because of their alleged depradations on game-bird chicks and poultry. By the turn of last century pine martens were almost exterminated over their main ranges, surviving in small pockets in the Lake District, in the Snowdon area of north Wales, in south-west Ireland, with their main last stronghold confined between Ardnamurchan and Cape Wrath, mainly in west Sutherland and Wester Ross. The slaughter relaxed in the First World War when most able bodied men were after targets of a different kind. In the late 1920s and 1930s they began to multiply again slowly, gaining another respite in the Second World War when they spread to Loch Ness and were found south of it by 1961. The new conifers planted by the Forestry Commission and private interests later helped martens considerably so their numbers slowly swelled in other isolated pockets too. Today they are found in all counties of the north and west Highlands. They were also helped by being protected, along with otters and wildcats, in the Wildlife and Countryside Act of 1981, for which I and other conservationists had long been campaigning.

I was delighted when I took my first flash-light photo of the marten on my bird table. Martens are omnivorous feeders but the bulk of their food consists of field voles and mice. Small birds and their eggs are next and a few young hares and rabbits are also taken. They eat large quantities of berries in summer and autumn, as well as beetles, large insects, small fish and carrion from dead deer in winter. But the one food they cannot resist is raspberry jam on buttered bread! At first I put out whole slices which the marten quickly grabbed and ran off before I could push the camera button. I learnt to cut the slices into small squares so the marten had to hang about to go from one to the other.

I also put heavy rooted wefts of moss over the bird table, to make a more natural looking background.

In the end the marten became so tame he came through my study window and
took food from my hand and, after the first year, even from my mouth.

When a great tit killed itself by flying into the window I put it on my desk along with the raspberry squares. The marten took two of the jammy squares before he took the birds.

In the second year the marten brought along his new mate, and at first she was a little shy of coming through the window. In the first snowstorm hunger made her bolder and she came in by her mate's side. When, later, they brought their kids too I once had five pine martens on my desk and they let me briefly stroke them as they darted about for the jammy squares, just showing slight resentment or fear by giving little huffy 'chrem' growls.

Field voles often raised my moss covered bird table for food left by the birds. Oddly, they remained unmolested by the pine martens.

Two young hares or 'leverets' in their birth 'form' crouch down hoping they have not been seen. As yet their ears are not longer than their heads which they will be when adult.

BUTTERFLIES

Gaudy dark-green fritillary butterflies flitted and glided among the white tops of pignut, the golds and oranges of ragwort, tormentil, bog asphodel, bird's foot trefoil, and the dark-blue chips of milkwort flowers. But among them all, hard to see with their jerky, wispy flight were hosts of scarce checkered skippers, a butterfly so rare it is given special protection under the Wildlife and Countryside Act of 1981. Over the years I had planted and encouraged their food plants, and now I was reaping a full reward. One landed on a late bluebell before me, holding its forewings, with their delicate patterns of yellow-gold plates, stiffly upwards, its rear wings drooped in true skipper fashion. I took some rare photos.

Fritillary butterflies trying to mate: The lower one is a male dark-green fritillary but while I have a book illustrating fifty fritillary species, I was unable to identify the large upper one, so it must be rare.

A red admiral on a buddleia bush flower which I planted in the front meadow.

The common blue is no longer common in the Highlands, so I was always pleased to see any around my remote homes.

A rare great grey shrike was a winter visitor to the Borders forest in which I was then living.

COMMON SEALS

One hot day in May I went to photograph the seals. They lay on the rocks, with their wedge-shaped flippers sticking out or closely tucked into their sides, like great shiny moles with snub, upturned noses. Two of them were very fat as if about to give birth. Their colours varied greatly, the larger ones being blackish or mottled brown, while smaller younger ones ranged from light brown to yellowish to grey-white, and there was one marbled with dark grey and cream. All were common seals (a misnomer because the larger Atlantic seals are more common) and their attitudes and postures were hilarious. There was a large brown one that lay on its side like a huge sausage flipped from a pan, a black one on its back, eyes tightly closed, velvet brows furrowed like a bloodhound's as a slight bump in the rock pushed its upper neck skin forward. The small marbled grey one held one flipper straight up into the air as if saying 'Hi, I'm over here'. Two had their heads and rear flippers curved upwards as if doing back exercises. I could hear odd snorts, snuffs and digestive burps that sounded like growls. A noisy lot!

Common seal pups in Scotland are born in early June and the females are ready to mate about six weeks later. The pups are born on the haul-out islets or mud or sandbanks, can swim at birth, and suck their mother's rich milk for a month or longer, both above and below water.

SEASCAPE

It was idyllic, just sitting there out in the broad Atlantic, rod in my hand, with the lion couchant landscape of Eigg, the high mountains of Rhum and the small island of Muck shimmering out on the horizon The beauty was intense, blue and gold, enough to make the soul quiver. The blazing colours of the wonderful seascape seemed to drench my retina. Suddenly the rod tip shot under the water – I was into a shoal of mackerel and in minutes I had more than enough to keep fresh without a fridge. I rowed past where common seals had hauled out to bask in the sun on the islets and they hunched and slid into the water as usual. I cut a few of the fish into pieces and threw them in. To my delight the seals began diving and rolling at the surface after the easy food. I whistled and crooned to them and they seemed more curious than ever before. They popped their heads up and down, snorted, splashed their hind flippers on the surface, submerged and came up somewhere else blinking their soulful dewy eyes, and followed my boat all the way to my beach. As I glided between the marbled islets with their nefarious tribes of gulls, cormorants, ducks, vivid darting terns and brilliant oyster catchers, the seals splashing about me, it was as if I were indeed in paradise.

'It was idyllic, just sitting there fishing in the intense blue-gold beauty of that wonderful seascape' from *Between Earth and Paradise*.

Stalking the hills in summer is a sweaty business and I used camouflaged clothes soaked in boiled pine and spruce needle juice and smeared crushed bog myrtle leaves over face, hands and areas of clothes most prone to perspiration. I often found young red deer calves, born in late May and early June, lying alone in little clefts of the ground. It is wrong to believe they have been abandoned just because you can't see the mother hind. She stays with her calf the first day but as it grows stronger she often leaves it lying for long periods in the grass or among heather or bracken to go grazing. She may even wander as far as a mile away. Then, remembering where the calf is, comes back in the afternoon, gives a soft bleat and up gets the calf for more milk.

I was descending a steep ridge when suddenly, in a small niche in the grasses, head tucked between its little front hooves hoping it wouldn't be seen, there was a lovely dappled cream-spotted calf. I took four pictures as it shrank there, then fixing my eyes on a spot a foot away so they wouldn't meet the calf's gaze directly, I stole nearer, fully expecting it to get up and run. But it didn't, and I managed to gently hold it round the neck. Immediately it let out a piercing 'bleea!' and its little grey nostrils were dilating, its beautiful long lashes blinking slowly and fearfully over its huge eyes. Moving very slowly, I sat down and talked to it soothingly, stroking gently as it laid its head and neck across my legs and relaxed almost totally. I took another close photo, then got up carefully and let it go. It staggered away a few steps then turned and started coming back to me!

I had to be very firm, laid it down and made a hasty retreat. I caught another one in the same way, found two more but realised I had been wrong to touch them as my scent might put the mother off, and I never touched one again.

Trying to get near a group of hinds in an awkward cross wind, I saw further away a hind with two fawns at her heels coming upwards from the left. I fully expected another hind or two to be with her but when none came I realised these could just be twin calves, extremely rare among red deer. Heart thudding, I slid like a snake through the summer grasses and round tiny prominences until I was near enough for really good photos. Magic moments came – the fawns, smaller than others I'd seen, still had pretty white spots on their red-brown coats. They nuzzled each other, one chased the other on to a small hillock, they butted heads together, then one reared up on to its mother's back as if trying to mount her. The clouds scudded away from the sun giving me the nuances of light I had hoped for, I was then certain they were twin calves as both were familiar with the hind and all the others had gone out of sight over a ridge.

Red deer stags live in 'bachelor' herds through winter, spring and summer, usually on higher ground and away from the hind herds. In early August this sociable group of stags are in prime condition after summer feeding and are still in velvet, which will soon be shed as they get ready to split up and mate with the hinds in the autumn rut. These stags would be a stalker's dream but while it is legal to shoot stags in the Highlands from July 1st to October 21st, traditional stalking is not practised until the end of September when the rut starts, velvet long shed, the stags are at their best and are easier to stalk as they are on lower ground with the hinds and also distracted by the need to mate and keep their 'harems' of hinds together.

A healthy hind, with full red summer coat, and her six-week old calf.

By early autumn the hinds, yearlings and this year's calves are in top condition and the hinds are ready for the rut.

The first autumn storms and hail showers can act as a trigger upon the red deer in the hills for it is now the big master stags break away from the bachelor herds and may travel many miles, usually to favoured places, to find hinds they can round up into their rutting 'harems'. In the past few weeks the sex glands become stimulated, the mane grows, the neck thickens, antlers are hard and the stags find their voices. Each stag tries to round up as many hinds as possible and seeks to protect them from other stags and stop any from straying while mating with them.

WILDERNESS PHILOSOPHY

Coming back from the beach on a cold drizzly autumn day I found two buff-tailed bumble bees helplessly dying as they clung to the last purple knapweed flowers. I had never seen bees work harder, lurching from flower to sparse flower, even when other bees had just denuded the same flower of all nectar. Now, defeated by the cold and rain and age, they were still at work, probing their thick tongues painfully into flowers in dying slow motion. Such blind tragic dedication, it seemed. If only we could work like that, preserve in our own lives this god-like creative impulse.

Many times I saw newly hatched moths, unlucky enough to emerge on a stormy day, dashed to pieces on rocks by winds, or pinned upside down by gales and rain, wings smashed, having made only one brief pointless flight. I felt sad. When we trek the fields and hills how many creatures do we kill with a single step, without even knowing? But the world was made thus. There is an awful waste in nature, and if we are only part of nature, I felt, we are doomed. It often seemed to me that the western intellectual has become divorced from nature, like most of mankind, preaching homilies about a god of love, seemingly unaware of the harsh reality in the kingdoms of the wild. Surely it is man's duty to protect and enhance the last of the natural world. Animals are innocent. We have creative intelligence, foresight and the ability to love spiritually but abuse our privilege for short-term gain.

This stag left his hinds to pound towards where I lay behind a small rock. Up in the wild hills at these times one is aware that attacks on man, while rare, have occurred. I stood up, waved my jacket, and he fled!

The big stag began to roar. He walked to a small mound and with swelled neck and dark mane thrust out, he bellowed his first challenge across the green and golden hills. When the mountain slopes are filled with roarings it feels as if one is surrounded by unseen lions. I located different groups by directing my binoculars towards each roaring. I tried to decide which to stalk first so that, even if they ran after my final approach, they wouldn't alarm the deer groups ahead or run across the large shallow corrie for all to see. A photo-stalker has only done his job if he can photograph deer without them knowing he is there.

A master stag will sniff a standing hind to find out if she is ready to mate. When this one trotted smartly away he ran after her with his tongue out, trying to lick her rear, with a lips-raised leering look. Sometimes he stationed himself next to a sitting hind and nuzzled her neck, and two of them nuzzled him back but none of them got up to stand for him. Each time a hind slipped away from him he would give up after a brief chase, then pause to roar, his voice trailing off as if with frustration. Monarch of the glen? The hinds are the real bosses, grazing more or less when, how and where they wish, and the stag has to wait until they are ready to mate, which is usually no more than one day in twenty. And if one has stalked badly, it is a hind who spots or scents you, gives a short hoffing bark, and away goes the herd while the amorous stag, mind intent on other matters, gazes after them with surprise. Then he trots after them.

The stag trotted off to round up an errant hind with short grunting 'but but but' noises. With head extended, he looked like a huge horned dog, his whole body rippling with muscles. I could hear the loud pounding 'tum tum tum' of his piston hooves on the short, cropped turf of the hill. It was quite scary.

If the roarings and menacing runs at rivals don't turn the challenging beasts away stags will fight for possession of hind-harems. When the younger stag came too close the master stag on the right turned him then they walked along an invisible boundary as if the bigger one was just escorting his rival away. Then both turned towards each other, moved their heads away as if they'd thought better of it, then a swift turn in and CLASH! The battle was on. Stags don't jab and gouge like bulls but lock antlers, head to head, and strive to assert dominance by agility and strength. It sounded like a pair of giants jousting with hat wracks. Both withdrew slightly, as if setting their antlers better, clashed again then heaved and strained against each other, eyes rolling wildly, breath snorting, divots of earth flying up from the striving hooves. Finally the younger stag's legs began to buckle and he slipped, recovered, slipped again, then turned to flee. The big stag gouged at his rump for good measure as he ran off.

By early November, most of the master stags have come to the end of their rut. They stand for long periods with drooping heads as if dazed and are more tolerant towards the younger stags. I've seen tired old beasts lying down, eyes half closed, taking no notice of four or five-year old stags which amble past only twenty yards away. It's often believed the big stag is exhausted towards the end of the rut by the constant mating, but the truth is that it would be unusual for more than one or two hinds to be ready for him on any one day. It is as much the constant running about, chivvying the hinds, bellowing challenges to rivals, occasional fights, and the lack of interest in feeding that causes exhaustion.

Now the younger stags have their chance with the hinds and there is a more peaceful atmosphere, the roars are less frequent and higher in pitch. Fights are fewer and less violent and there is an air of amateurism. I have seen mature hinds, now well served by the masters, peevishly strike out with their forefeet at young swains who show too much interest. The amorous youngsters are eager but their lack of experience shows, and they often look most disgruntled when their approaches are rebuffed.

When winter lays its savage hand over the hills there is very little food for golden eagles, red deer or even foxes upon the high tops. And the wildlife trekker realises he is no nearer heaven by climbing a mountain!

A raven has pounced on a mouse or vole under the snow crust, and has left the marks of its flight feathers after the hard landing in the snow.

One false step in the icicle-filled crevasses over some burns and one would be away to a slithering, painful death.

A most tragic sight – an old stag with a rear foot wedged between rocks in an icy river.

After fording the river and avoiding his weak attempts to gouge me, I managed to haul him out by the antlers. But he just lay on the ground, eyes rolling, too weak to move further. It was terrible to see him there, his long graceful legs stretched out, his flank heaving, the great spread of antlers distorting the lying position of his head and pushing his muzzle into the ground. The fallen monarch. How many glens, how many miles had passed beneath those flying cloven hooves, how many peaks had he gained to see a world few humans ever see, how many harems had he herded together, hinds had he served, defended against other stags? How many times had he roared his challenge across the glens in the fall? How had he felt in his youthful prime when proud of his strength, proud of his speed, he had gazed with fearful disdain at the stalkers labouring below, for by heaven he had evaded them all? But now Time, the greatest stalker of all, had caught up with him, as it does with us all, the foolish, the clever, the weak or the strong.

wouldn't leave him like that, lying helplessly on his side. I went round to his rear and pushed him upright. As I reached under his belly to pull his lower leg so he would be lying naturally, he swung his head round and his right antler just missed my eye. I clutched the antler at the tip so he would have less leverage and forced his head against his body, then with all four feet correctly placed, I jumped back as I let go. He gazed at my departure in weak surprise for he must have thought he was going to be killed. When I got back from a long trek he had gone. I hoped he would survive but I doubted it.

CARING

When we care for a wild animal or bird it is essential to comprehend the creature's instincts, to behave in a way that will allay its fears and suspicions, cater to its dominant senses, and always to forgive its apparent lack of understanding. For wild animals are not underlings or inferior species. All too often we look at them through the arrogant screen of our own complicated and artificial lives, and so we see them falsely. We patronise them for their so-called lower existence, their ignorance, their unreasoning 'savagery', their inconvenient interference with humanity's headlong rush to gain its own comfort and pleasure at whatever cost to nature .... Mammals, birds, fish and insects exist in a far older and more perfect world than any we have been able to create for ourselves. These creatures live by instincts and senses we are fast losing or have never developed. They recognise natural rhythms to which we are no longer attuned, voices we cannot hear. They fulfil their roles as intended while we devote massive energy to attempts at escape. Over half of humanity is either starving or seriously under-nourished. For all our learning, inventive brilliance and individual genius, humanity on the whole has shown far less real survival instinct than a herd of red deer.

Mortality among red deer is common, especially if they don't get six weeks of fairly dry weather after the rut; the
go right down and seek woods at the bottoms of glens for shelter. The weaker ones stay there, too feeble to climb th
hills again. Warble fly larvae in their coats let the air in so they get colder and wetter. Nasal botfly grubs and lun
worms are common parasites. Severe infections of lung worms are very debilitating and as the animal gets weake
pneumonia develops, causing death. Mortality occurs mainly amongst the oldest and youngest animals. Here,
young stag has died on the loch shore and has been opened up by golden eagles, typically behind the ribs to get c
lungs and heart.

It is not often one finds such clea.
and clinical flensing of a carcas
and it is sometimes mistaken fc
the work of escaped pumas o
other big cats. But I found th
to be done by a pair of badger.
rolling back the skin and fur to ge
more efficiently at the meat.

It is not all doom and gloom, however. Death among wild animals is natural in the winter wilds, and the decaying carcasses release vital nutrients to the soil. Around them in the spring the herbage is lusher, greener than elsewhere. There seems more to the old adage 'from dust to dust, ashes to ashes'. In nature there is no waste. All flesh is grass and back to grass goes the flesh.

I hauled a dead roebuck up to 600 feet just above my wild cottage, hoping to get the golden eagle pair down so I could photograph and film them. Hooded crows and ravens came first but it was eight days before the eagles trusted the situation. Here, the female eagle patiently waits while her smaller mate rends the carrion.

The female's greater size and strength were obvious when she began to heave the 32 lb roebuck carcass uphill. I filmed her tramping down to it, lifting her huge pantalooned yellow feet high over the grasses. Then she bounced on down a a gawky run, wings flapping slightly to maintain balance. She put one foot high up on the buck and peered down as if working out how best to tackle it, the sun glinting like fire in her fierce eyes. No flesh was showing so she removed her foot again, braced both sets of talons below the roebuck's backbone, grabbed the skin at the a edge of the small hole the ravens and male had made by the ribcage, and heaved. Now she really meant business. I was more in awe than ever at her sheer power, the strength in her back and neck. Heave, heave, HEAVE … each jerk repeated quickly after the one before. With her feet climbing backwards, wings beating for more force, she lifted the entire carcass right off the ground and hauled it more than a yard uphill! It was an astonishing feat to witness, and to film, for what was left of the corpse must still have weighed over 30 lbs, three times her own weight. To me, she was more like a winged tiger than a bird .. I had six minutes of film that would astonish the world!

A golden eagle's eyrie ledge at 1, 200 feet midway up a natural 'chimney'. I have studied eagles for 40 years but at first I made many mistakes, searching for eyries at over 2,000 feet over 300 square miles of west Highland mountains, reasoning that the bird would want to be far from man! In fact the average height of 30 eyries was 1,013 feet. Needing to often carry quite heavy prey to the nest to feed eaglets, they don't want to have to always fly up. Flying level or even down from hunting on the high tops makes much more sense.

MOUNTAIN LANDSCAPE

I never climbed the mountains just to reach their tops, but to discover their wildlife secrets. I had known these Highland mountains would be a hard world to really come to know. I had to learn that these miles of wild open hills, so different in every season, had to be approached like mysterious, even desirable, gods, to whose secrets one would never gain access without patient perseverance, a certain stealth and cunning, and above all love. Spring, nature's boast, was the alluring nymphet, summer the mature but capricious goddess, autumn the crotchety god losing his prime, and winter a vicious old god of withered skin and frozen bones; and that while all their secrets were revealed but slowly they would be worth all the more for that.

BUZZARDS

It is in late March that spring always strings two or three cloudless days together, the sun burning down from heaven's blue vault with pure heat on the cold-gripped earth, and I keep my eyes – and ears – open for the courtship of the great buzzards. 'Kee-oo' comes the high-pitched ringing cry above the silent hills, echoing between the two woods, and being thus kindly warned of their coming, I dash for my camera to try to secure better flying pictures of these fine birds of prey, second only in size to the golden eagle. Buzzards are really small eagles and I often feel they should be called the Woodland Eagle, although they do often 'perch-hunt' from telegraph poles, which no golden eagle would ever do. They are probably now our most common bird of prey for in recent years they have spread south to most counties and there are estimated to be over 3,000 pairs in the UK.

I often witness their spring courtships on the wing. Two smaller males will fly with the large female competing for her attention but not fighting each other. I've seen the true pair bond asserted when one cock makes a strong display, raising wings high, flapping very slowly, and bringing them down below his body each time as he gains height. Then he dives on to the hen, who turns sideways with talons out, as if expressing her preference among the two males. Then the two birds make tight circles round each other, at times almost beak to beak, both calling loudly 'kee-oo' ... 'king-oo' ... 'kee-oo' ... 'king-oo' and the discomfited second suitor drifts away alone.

When the morning sun reflecting from the loch lights them from below, I am surprised at the sheer beauty and myriad colours of their underwings: whites, buffs, greys, browns, and ruddy flames of orange feathers arranged in superbly intricate patterns. The buzzard is not just a mottled brown old bird.

The cliff containing the eyrie at the end of the 'killer trek' which consisted of eight hard miles with 12,000 feet of ups and downs, sometimes with a film gear pack weighing 64 lbs.

This is eagle country – the dizzying but spectacular view from beside an eagle's eyrie. One wrong step here and one would be away to a bouncing, scraping death.

Eagles usually lay two eggs between mid March and mid April, and I have seen them stoically incubating eggs with snow all around them and even on them. Courtship begins in December and both birds build up nests, sometimes as many as three before deciding on the final eyrie, the female doing most of the building. She does most of the incubating too, though the male will relieve her for short periods. Eggs hatch in 40 to 44 days and the bigger chick from the first laid egg is more successful in the competition for food, and will harrass and attack its smaller sibling which usually dies. Out of 62 known nesting attempts by ten pairs of golden eagles that I monitored over ten years, 42 succeeded in raising a total of 45 eaglets to flying stage. Only three pairs raised twin eagles successfully, one pair achieving this twice.

A three-week old eaglet, still clad in white down, will show some resistance to a human intruder. The mother spends most of her time around the nest up to this time, brooding the chick at night and in cold weather, and feeding it from prey brought in by the male. She will make short hunting spells herself on fine warm days.

A five-week old eaglet, its bulging white crop showing that it has been well fed. At this age an eaglet is well capable of rending its own food from the prey brought in by its parents.

The eyrie bathed in golden sunlight at dawn. 'Heaven's morning breaks, and earth's vain shadows flee …' What a magical sight the mother now presented. The sun danced the browns, fawns, russets and golds of her feathers into flaming lights. I was impressed by the sheer majesty and quietness of her, the dignified aristocratic mien, the massive chest and shoulders and thick neck, arched at the back like a fighting bull's, the wide head and strong blue-black beak. The whole impression was one of nobility and serene power.

As probably the only person to clock up over 3,000 hours in eagle hides and to spend many nights out on precarious cliff ledges to see what eagles get up to in darkness, I was amazed to witness many examples of a female eagle's genuine affection for her chick. I once wrote: 'There is no love or compassion in the animal world, only maternal, and occasionally paternal, care – and even that is short-lived.' But I could at times have sworn the mother eagle did 'love' her bairn and the obvious rapport between them was overwhelming. She often gave the impression of immense calm and reserved power. The great cruiser of the skies stilled at last, as if in a painting by Millais. Once she lifted her head and yawned sleepily with her beak wide open, and the eaglet, seeing this, caught the urge too and yawned in the same way.

... was just in time to photograph the male eagle landing with talons out, primary feathers all separated from each ... ther before the wings folded, with a sprig of heather in his beak. I will never forget the chick's look of disappointment, ...'s crop empty, its eyes fixed on the inedible sprig.

'... 's that all you can bring, Dad? I'm damn well starving!'

Eagles bring in sprays of foliage and vegetation for several reasons I found: They can act as pair bonding 'gifts'
for decoration of the nest (fox gloves were once brought to a nest) and mainly to freshen up nests where small bits
of meat and bone are not carried away by the female and the sprays are trodden down on top of them. I've seen
eagles bring in hefty sprays and set them down on the windward side of the nest as if to shelter the chick. It is most
annoying when this action blocks my camera's view of the chick! I have seen chicks using the sprays to wipe their
beaks after messy feeding and also, when lying down for a rest, using them to brush away flies and biting midges
from their heads and necks.

A well grown, quarter-eaten fox cub on an eagle's eyrie. From a distance I saw the female eagle clearly spy the fox cub amid white-wooled lamb legs outside its rocky den while soaring. She had deliberately lost height fast, then gone into a rapid glide behind the rocks – to thump down onto the fox and kill it when it could not have seen her coming. I have found seven dead foxes on eagle nests. If the sheep farmers' estimate that in Lochaber one fox family kills an average of eight lambs per season is correct, and these seven foxes had each raised just two families in its lifetime, the eagles indirectly 'saved' the lives of over one hundred lambs.

Although the eaglet had been tearing and gulping down pieces of a curlew perfectly well on its own, when its mother came in it flapped its wings, lowered its beak and began squeaking, demanding to be fed. She showed it the real way to feed. She crept towards the curlew like a huge manacled cat, struck it a blow with one set of talons, then with a simple easy snip and tweak pulled a big lump off, lifted it up and twisting her head sideways delicately fed it to the eaglet. She always presented food to her chick with exaggerated care. At last I had a fine sideways feeding shot with both birds' heads in good profile.

After seven weeks eaglets often do high overhead what I call 'hottentot' stretches with their wings to help strengthen them.

WILDERNESS PHILOSOPHY

From *Golden Eagle Years* (Written in 1981)

The winter that ensued was the coldest, snowiest but also the driest I had so far known in the Highlands, but after making a cottage heater from a forty-four gallon oil drum, an invention learned from an old Scots-Indian in Canada, I passed it in more comfort than usual, despite having to spend a whole day each week cutting and hauling dead logs. I wasn't seeing the local eagles on winter treks now. Rather than sit and mope on Christmas Day I set out with Moobli on the hardest hike for weeks. I always felt better after hard exertion on the Hill, and if it is true that a man is partly what he eats and partly what he thinks, it also helped my mental processes. We headed along the loch shore, up a long river valley, then turned to climb a steep killer of a hill to over 1,700 feet. I had to cling on to dwarf trees to get up some of the almost sheer faces.

We emerged on to the peak and there below us lay a vast expanse of undulating-tawny hills, precipitous crags and high cliffs, the loch winding like a silver scarf between them to the sun-filled west. On the steep slopes, herds of red deer blended with russet clumps of dead bracken, barely distinguishable but for their white-buff rump patches. I saw the two adult eagles heading towards us and Meleager banked, climbed and dived down by Atalanta's side, so close to us that I heard the wind rushing through his pinions. The whole scene was so wonderful it took the rest of my breath away. What a privilege it was to be up there among nature at its wildest. Without the ability to appreciate such beauty and the desire to work towards conserving it, I thought, man is little more than a beast.

Here I was once more on the roof of the world, amid timelessness, mystery, the unknown, and ancient silence, as if I were standing in the real 'cathedral of God'. We have suffered from loosening our roots in the natural world and losing the sense of wonder, deepened intuition and percep-tion that naturally occur when we see nature's most extraordinary and beautiful phenomena. We are humbled by such glimpses of glorious creation and the mind opens, the soul becomes inspired at last. I felt then that our final attitude to the last of the natural world is an important barometer of our state of mind as a species. We humans evolved from original creation with su-perior gifts of intelligence, foresight, communal invention and the unique ability to love spir-itually beyond ourselves, to become the world's most dominant species. Yet each dominant spe-cies before us perished when it could not adapt to changing conditions. Today it is we who are changing environmental conditions, often to our own detriment, and at a pace with which many habitats cannot cope.

Eleven civilisations before ours foundered when they cut their roots to the land, lost awareness of universal nature, and affluence bred decadence; thus it has long proved insufficient to dominate alone. Animals have no choice beyond survival but man does have choice and he must use his unique gifts now to play the role for which he has truly evolved, as responsible custodian of the last wild places, not merely their exploiter. We can never escape the inherent responsibility our genius bestows upon us. We must learn to love and conserve what is inspiring and beautiful, not only what is economically profitable.

As I walked on, the certainty came that if we do not exercise that choice, help to transfigure the callous side of nature, so often reflected in our own natures, by compassion and acts of intelligent conversation, we will begin to die spiritually – are not the signs now all around us? – and then create a hell on earth for ourselves before we too pass along the route to extinction. We shall be yet another of Gods failed species (if we believe in God), just another failure of evolution (if we do not). To love in the universal sense is not the refuge-seeking philosophy of the romantic. It is the necessary ethic of our own survival.

Eagles will hunt in pre-dawn and pro-dusk semi darkness where a trekking human has to be careful where he puts his feet. They will also hunt in rain if the chick needs food. Here, the mother eagle looks as scrawny as a vulture after hard unsuccessful hunting in the rain.

As I climbed up to take photos, the eight-week old eaglet hissed, raised his well-feathered wings in threat display and tried to drive me back with hard forward flaps. With head reared high, beak open and tongue upraised, he looked like a hooded cobra about to strike. Although I put my hand on the nest, he never tried to strike it with his talons.

A nine-week old eaglet watches enviously as its parent flies away.

A formidable sight (imagine being a rabbit!) as the mother eagle flies towards the hidden camera.
Again the eaglet watches with seeming envy; it's bored after so long on the high cliff nest.

Even at ten weeks, when it could now fly, an eaglet can still be fed by its mother.

When almost ready to fly young eagles do a great deal of 'trampolining' about the nest, flapping furiously and leaping from one side to the other, frantically clutching at the twigs to stop themselves going over the edge.

They also grab a firm hold of the main nest twigs and flap powerfully against the clutch of their talons. All this exercise serves to strengthen the wing muscles.

When the young eagle is ready to fly the parents mount a judicious 'starvation' technique and fly past the nest, often with food in their talons, to tempt it out. I would hear great wings going 'wush WUSH wush' past the hide and eyrie every half an hour, the eaglet would crouch down, give a rising volume of squeaks and flap its wings trying to solicit her into the nest. She would zoom past close to the nest then go onto an oblong path along the opposite ridges and back again. She seemed to be showing the youngster this is how you do it, this is how you fly, this is what you have to do yourself before long if you want food.

After seeing his mother in the distance with prey in her talons, the young eagle bravely charges across the nest for its first flight.

Three days later the young eagle flew past the nest, saw me and sailed closer for a better look, giving me a good flight picture from above her.

A rare picture of successful twin eagle chicks in their eyrie and now almost ready to fly. The male eaglet watches his sister exercising her wings and trampolining.

The male eagle seemed to hang in the air as he sailed in with a headless ptarmigan in his talons.

She looked immense and dark against the blue of the sky, her great wings beating slowly but powerfully, eyes glaring from her wide wedge-shaped head. I felt an inner tremor at the close spectacle of evolution's natural dark angel of death.

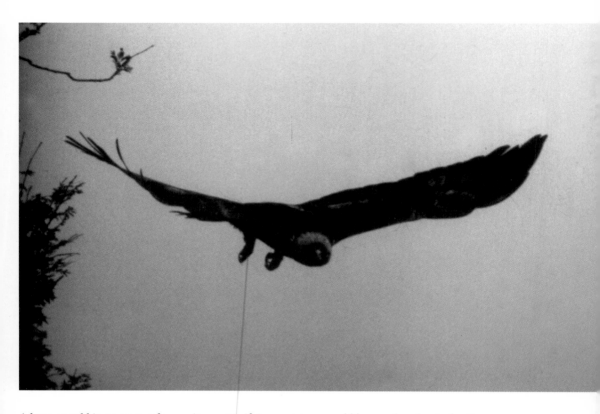

A hare or rabbit, or even a fox, seeing so terrifying a vision, would be paralysed out of action.

Keeping the nest clean, the female eagle leaped away with a desiccated red deer calf's foreleg in her beak.

After leaving half a rabbit on the eyrie, the male eagle jumped into the windless air and beat away with dangling talons, his beak still open in the July heat.

The mother eagle had been in the nest beside her chick for twenty hours and the male came in, lifted his wings twice, wanting her to have a 'float' with him as he had already seen the nest had a full larder of prey and the chick was well fed. She wasn't going, however, and seemed to communicate to him that she needed some fresh foliage to screen the chick. He flew off and returned (here) with a bare stick. She took it from him, dropped it in apparent disgust and gave him another meaningful look. Something was communicated.

Understanding her demand for better foliage, he crouched, jumped and beat away. He landed on the rock beside m
hide and I heard his great talons scratching its surface. My heart thudding with excitement, I heard a brief brushin
noise, the roof of the hide sank slightly, rose again and then there was a loud 'tunk' sound as if something had bee
tugged free. Then came a loud woofing of wings, rapidly receding. I got to the viewer just in time to see him landin
back on the nest – with a big heather spray he had tugged from the roof of my hide as the female arranged a birc
twig round the chick.

he picked up the big heather spray like a banner bearer, then stepped across the chick and across the nest with
xaggerated care.

Then she wove it into the nest in front of the chick, almost hiding it from my view. It was astonishing to thus witness the apparently silent communication between the two great birds.

The male shot in again, this time with a leafy rowan spray, which he tucked behind the eaglet. He gave her a look as if to say 'Okay! Now we can go!'.

Only then would she fly off the nest to join him in the air, no doubt feeling her chick was safely screened. But the chick stood up!

n my third year I got my best shot of an eagle with its chick so far, with the male standing high and proud, with a *eather sprig in his beak. His eyes were bigger in proportion to his head than the female's. He was a smaller, lighter- *oloured bird but really sleek and strong, his legs thickly muscled.

SURVIVAL

If I was finding it hard to survive in wilderness winters in a cottage without any mod cons, how must it feel to be an ageing eagle? What was it like, after a life based on physical prowess, when the eyes were no longer keen enough to spot the white blob of a sitting ptarmigan on the high tops, the speed no longer there to pursue and catch the dodging rabbit or hare, and when the talons lost their killing strength? How to cope when the only hope of survival in the bleak winter was to stay aloft on those great wings which, although fashioned by evolution to carry her for hour upon hour without a single beat, were now beginning to tire? How must it feel to know you have to kill something before you can have breakfast?

VHS Videos from Mike Tomkies

EAGLE MOUNTAIN YEAR (125 minutes, £18)

This tape tells the story of a magical Highland mountain through all four seasons. There are golden eagles at the nest, their glorious courtship 'air dances', and a female eagle hauling a deer carcass uphill on her own. Rare black-throated divers are seen diving, courting and, for the first time on film, at their nest. Pine martens are shown hunting, at their den, even feeding from my hands. Hunting and nesting peregrine falcons are shown in detail, as is all the comic-tragic sibling rivalry at buzzard nests. There are courting mergansers, ospreys, ravens, foxes and even a hunting wildcat. Throughout all, I show the lives of the red deer herds.

AT HOME WITH EAGLES (102 minutes, £16)

Shown in incredibly intimate detail, this is the story of three pairs of courting, hunting and nesting golden eagles – one pair exchanging incubation duties, a second pair trying against the odds to hatch infertile eggs, and a third pair who are successful in raising their chick from egg to flying stage. Never before have the secret lives of the king of birds been revealed in such fascinating detail. Two eminent naturalists have described it as probably the greatest eagle film ever made.

FOREST PHANTOMS (60 minutes, £9)

This tape takes six barn owls through a full year, from chicks to hunting adults. Also starred are the forest phantoms of the day – rare goshawks at the nest, as well as nesting buzzards, long-eared owls, foxes, and, yes, even eagles again.

MY BARN OWL FAMILY (52 minutes, £9)

A tape of my barn owls Blackie and Brownie, and how they finally raised four young-sters to flying stage. We see them incubating eggs, hunting the woods and pastures, perch hunting from my garden fence, and taking prey back up to the loft. Intimate glimpses of their complicated behaviour inside the loft and nest box; and all the growing stages of the chicks are recorded in loving detail. Also shown are the daytime 'invaders' of their world – a badger who was unusually tame, a fox who used my sheep walls to spy prey, a beautiful female kestrel who came for any food the owls left on the table – not to mention chaffinch hordes, bellicose siskins, cheeky jays and other entrancing characters.

RIVER DANCING YEAR (92 minutes, £13)

A celebration of the superb wildlife of Scottish rivers – from the raging upper water-falls where salmon leap heroically to reach their spawning grounds; through serene reaches where swans, herons, moorhens, mallards, dippers, goosanders, gulls and kingfishers go about their lives and finally to where the river enters the sea and the estuary kingdom of the great sea eagles. We see foxes playing in a riverside garden, a vixen giving suck to her four cubs … a boisterous badger family, digging, playing hilarious judo games, and even taking food from my hands … a grooming, prowling and hunting wildcat … otters fishing and in their holt … peregrines guarding their chicks … herons catching fish and even swallowing a duckling, a young golden eagle preparing to leave its nest … ospreys catching and bringing fish to their grown young … and a host of other species. Above all, it is a long insight into the world of the rare white-tailed sea eagles, as a pair guard their flown youngster, exchange beak-to-beak greetings, and provide glorious flight sequences when they hunt for prey in their kingdom at the end of the river.

WILDEST SPAIN (77 minutes, £10)

A tape about Europe's finest wildlife. It tells of successful treks and adventures all over Spain in pursuit of wild bear, wolf, lynx, wild boar, ibex, black stork, very rare vultures and eagles, plus many other species in a magical European country not hitherto known for its often excellent wildlife conservation.

WILDEST SPAIN REVISITED (52 minutes, £9)

This updates the previous video, with totally new material, concentrating on rare wild brown bear and wild wolves. Some extraordinary and hitherto unknown behaviour is captured.

LAST EAGLE YEARS (75 minutes, £10)

This tape covers the five wilderness years since all the previous videos ended. I show three pairs of hunting, courting and nesting golden eagles, a veritable feast of red kites competing with ravens, buzzards and crows for food, and goshawks and peregrine falcons at the nest. There are wild goats (and a fight between two males), brown hares, courting curlews, red and rare black-throated divers, and a long sequence of ospreys hunting for fish and feeding young at two nests. On my way to the kingdom of the rare white-tailed sea eagles, I show huge Atlantic seals and dolphins somersaulting in the sea, and finally the great sea eagles soaring to and from their island nest as they tend their single youngster.

MY BIRD TABLE THEATRES (80 minutes, £9)

This tape showing the fascinating behaviour of the myriad hordes of birds who visited bird tables at my last four homes, ranging from the wild Scottish hills near Ullapool, to the Borders and deepest Sussex. Shown through the four seasons, all the normal garden birds are here plus nuthatches, linnets, goldfinches, ring doves, colourful jays, green woodpeckers, comical squirrels, a flock of pheasants who became tame, and even a kestrel and a barn owl. At night foxes and a pair of badgers come for the food

I set out, including a huge semi-albino boar weighing over 30lbs who pulls down a Victorian pedestal a man can hardly lift, to get at some meat.

MY WILD 75th SUMMER (80 minutes, £9)

My last season filming peregrine falcons, red kites and goshawks feeding chicks at the nest; the roe deer, foxes and cubs, and a badger pair at my new wildlife reserve in deepest Sussex. It shows how I set up the reserve, planted a wild flower meadow and the butterflies it attracted. I show the playful and courting behaviour of rabbits, foxes, squirrels, pheasants, plus jays feeding flown chicks, a frolicking weasel and colourful woodpeckers. The film ends with fabulous footage of rare white-tailed sea eagles soaring to and from their tree nest on Mull with prey, and how they cooperate to feed their twin chicks. This 11-minute sequence, shot on my 76th birthday, is my 'swan song' to wildlife filming.

Books

GOLDEN EAGLE YEARS (£10)

The reissue of the book long out of print, which contains more and better colour pictures than the first edition. It tells of my first five years studying Scotland's magnificent golden eagles. The treks, the pitfalls and defeats, the joys and triumphs, are fully described.

ON WING AND WILD WATER (£10)

Superior Cape paperback of my second eagle book.

(All above prices of books and videos include first class post and packing, and please indicate if and how you want them signed. Cheques payable to Mike Tomkies)

Please send your remittance and delivery address to:

Whittles Publishing Ltd, Dunbeath Mains Cottages, Dunbeath, Caithness, KW6 6EY, Scotland.